From D
LIGHT

Poetic words of wisdom to help
your inner light shine bright

Elizabeth Vincenty

BookLeaf
Publishing
India | USA | UK

From DARK to LIGHT © 2024 Elizabeth
Vincenty

All rights reserved.

Presentation by *BookLeaf Publishing*

Web: www.bookleafpub.com

E-mail: info@bookleafpub.com

ISBN: 9789360946685

First edition 2024

DEDICATION

First and foremost, I dedicate this book to my beautiful mother, who was the first person to tell me that I should "write a book one day" shortly before she passed away. She was the absolute best mom that I could have ever asked for! I love you mom! Look! I did it! Thank you for always encouraging me to be myself, loving me the way you did and teaching me how to love myself and others! You may be gone from this earth but you're always in my heart and you will never be forgotten! I miss you every day! I love you forever and always!

I would also like to dedicate this book to my precious baby girls, Adrianna and Elisa! Mommy loves you both so incredibly much! Thank you for your beautiful loving smiles that I look forward to each day! I don't know what I would do without you! You are my world! Your positive energy gives me so much strength and your unconditional love makes me feel so alive. God bless you both! I thank God for you every day! I'm so honored to be your mom! I love you my girls! Always and forever! I'm so proud of you both and I want you to always remember that you are fearfully and

*wonderfully made, you are more than
enough and you are worthy of all your
dreams and happiness. May you always
remember that mommy loves you. I am
forever inside your heart and in the very
same blood that runs through your veins.
We are forever connected. May you always
find strength in remembering who you are
and how much you are loved. When life
seems to be dark, remember you have what
it takes inside of your heart to spark a
flame and bring light into the darkness.*

*This book is also dedicated to my best
friend Jaymie! My strength when I am weak
and the voice I can rely on when I cannot
speak. I love you girl! Thank you for always
being there for me! Thank you for loving me
unconditionally! Thank you for always
being real with me and thank you for just
being the beautiful soul that you are!*

**For all the broken hearts and tears ever shed!
In this generation and every next one ahead!
May each of you release the pain that you hold.
Love yourself first! You're worth more than gold.**

ACKNOWLEDGEMENT

For the accomplishment of this book, for the gift of life itself and for the opportunity to share my love and light with the world, I humbly and wholeheartedly give all my praise, honor and glory to God.

Thank you God for not only blessing my spirit with life on this earth but also for the opportunity to be a beacon of light in this world. May the words I have poured out from my soul reach the hearts of many and lift their spirits when needed. May the love and light that I have within me shine through the cracks of my heart and provide illumination for others during their times of emotional darkness. May the positive energy that I exude through my inner being inspire others and may my footsteps leave a blazing trail for others to follow so that they may find their way out from the darkness and back into the light.

PREFACE

The words in this book are poems from diaries and journals that I have gotten myself lost in over the years. Writing has always been one of my main passions and it has been my main source of therapy since I was a small child.

In the poems I've chosen to share, you will get a glimpse of my past, a peek into my current life and a sense of how I embrace the future. As in the title of this book, *From Dark to Light*, you will sense the energy of my words transition from dark to light. The poems range from feelings felt during times of emotional darkness and struggle to the days I found my inner light once again.

My journey of life has been a mixture of ups and downs with sudden twists and turns but I have learned to believe that with a heart full of love and an optimistic perspective on life, we can turn every negative situation into a positive learning experience and truly make our lives a great joy.

At times, heartbreak and pain can fill our eyes with tears that we are unable to see clearly. Our thoughts fill with dark fog during times of distress making us unable to think clearly. The darkness suddenly feels darker by the minute while the thought of love and light quickly fade from our grasp making it all seem like a mere dream... I know this to be true firsthand from the personal life experiences I have endured in my own journey. I have overcome a tremendous path of my own and after suffering in a cocoon of darkness for so long, I have finally emerged like a butterfly. I grew and learned how to handle life's trials and tribulations with greater strength and see the positive in all things as much as possible. Best of all, with a change of perspective, I learned one of life's greatest secrets to happiness and that is how to wake up each morning with a heart full of gratitude.

Nevertheless, while the unknown remains uncertain and the future remains a mystery, it still looks beautiful through the windows of my soul. Despite the storms of life that I may still encounter, I will remain resilient and continue to spread my wings out to fly with confidence as I face the world with faith and a humble heart of love and light each and every day.

May my words be used to change the world in a positive way and may the light inside my heart endlessly burn bright as I embody the essence of love and become the best version of myself that I can be; so that I can continue to make the rest of my life the best of my life, while helping others do the same.

Time In Darkness
Is Painful

Hidden

I can't seem to explain
The conflicts that I feel
I'm kind of lost for words
Tired of my own shpiel

All bottled up inside
My emotions start to pile
I can't explain why
So I hide behind a smile

Not a single soul
Knows just how I feel
Don't want any pity
Just want them to be real

I seem to be depressed
Too much on me, mentally
Won't get into the rest
Because it might be jealousy

So hidden behind my smile
I deal with my own ways
All my problems I seem to file
Hoping to forget them within days

Flowers

If April showers
Bring May flowers
Will all my tears
Create great hours

Will all my pain
Turn into power
Or will it make me
Be bitter and sour

I want to bloom
Like a beautiful rose
I want to feel tingles
From my head to my toes

I want to be picked
And placed in a vase
Feel the admiration
For my beautiful face

I want to be held
With honor and grace
Please water me daily
And give me a place

God, please save me!
Let the sky rain
Help me to bloom
Despite all my pain!

Thumps

I feel my heart racing
It's pounding so hard
My hands are now sweating
That caught me off guard

I didn't expect that
Don't know what to do
Except turn my face
I cannot look at you

How could you do this
You said you would never
You said you would love me
Always and forever

My heart was all yours
It beat only for you
Now it just thumps
Please, say it's not true

You were my whole world
It was us till the end
Now my heart's broken
I've lost my best friend

Silence

Stuck in a silence
Turning a blind eye
My body feels numb
My eyes are now dry

What will it take
To feel happy again
I need to have fun
I miss my best friend

I miss who I was
When I wasn't sad
All this is my fault
It makes me so mad

So mad at myself
I should have known better
I've always been strong
A determined go-getter

But now I feel weak
My heart cannot take it
I'm doing my best
To be happy and not fake it

Life

This really sucks
Life feels so unfair
I am to the point
Where I really do not care

So many bad things
Keep stealing my attention
And I'm a good person
With only good intention

I'm loyal and I'm honest
And I'm good to everyone
Yet bad things keep happening
To me and I am done

It makes me really wonder
Is God there, on my side?
Because all I want to do
Is run away and go hide

Orphan

I feel like I'm an orphan
Losing both my mom and dad
I don't say this for your pity
Even though I feel so sad

I wish life was like a dream
But it's more like a nightmare
Every day when I wake up
Nothing seems to ever compare

To the love that I once felt
When my parents were still here
No matter what I ever needed
Their love erased my every fear

But now with them both gone
I find myself all on my own
I'm so grateful for them both
And their love that was once shown

They both did the best they could
With what they had and what they knew
I just wish this wasn't real
Because their absence is so true

I can't wait for the sweet day
When God has us reunite
But until that day arrives
I cry myself to sleep at night

Dear Mom

Dear mom, if you can hear me
Please send a sign my way!
I really need to see you!
Can you visit me today?

When I lay down to sleep,
please meet me in my dreams!
I can't wait to see you!
I am bursting at the seams!

I'm so filled with excitement!
I have such good news to share!
I bet you will be proud of me!
For me you always cared.

Gosh I miss those feelings,
from the bond that we both had.
I hate it that you died so young!
Sometimes I get so mad.

Most of all what I am feeling,
Is so sad, so lost and alone.
I wish that I could see you, Mom,
or just call you on the phone.

But neither is an option,
So I can't have either one.
All I can do is write to you,
until my race is run.

Never Gone

I miss you so much
But I know you're never gone
You are here inside my heart
And you're in my favorite song

You're in everything around me
Everything brings thoughts of you
Sometimes I swear I hear your voice
But I know that it's not true

I feel so lost without you
But I know I must live on
I just have a broken heart
Now from me that you're gone

I mean, yeah I know, not really
You're not gone from me completely
The essence of your beautiful soul
Remains alive so discreetly

Knock on the Door

There was a sudden knock,
A loud banging on the door.
With dark eyes there she was!
Three kids, some bags, no more!

The look on all their faces,
And the tears in their sad eyes,
It said all that was needed,
Now no longer could she hide.

They quickly ran inside.
It was the one place she felt safe.
The trauma inside her eyes,
Proved with him, she was unsafe.

Before she could get settled,
There was a loud knock on the door.
There he was, asking for her!
Like it was her that he cared for!

But he only cared for himself!
Him and his green and hazel eyes.
He was the worst thing that she found!
He was the devil in disguise!!

He put her through the worst.
He made her fearful for her life.
He tried to win her with his charm,
But all he gave her was AIDS and strife!

Reflection

The world is full of people
Yet I feel so all alone
There's no one I can trust
So I talk to my own phone

Maybe Siri is my friend
She knows so much about me
She hears me when I cry
Never making me feel angry

The only friend I have
Is the girl in my reflection
She's the only one
The one and only true exception

She loves me just for me
And she holds me when I cry
She understands my pain
She's much nicer than a guy

She knows all my secrets
Yet she loves me just the same
Been with me all my life
Helping me not go insane

She smiles when I can't
And she sings out from my soul
She's been working very hard
To patch up every hole

From bullet wounds to stabs
So many cracks and holes to heal
The kind of love she gives
Feels so good cause it's called real

Through The Journey Remain Hopeful

Mourning

I'm grieving and I'm mourning
And I'm trying to self-heal
I am angry, I am crying
Trying to grow through what I feel

But the type of pain that comes
With this type of inner growth
It's too much for one to bear
But I stay true to my oath

May all the pain I go through
Be the payment for my light
May the light that shines through me
Help out others in their fight

May this light I have inside
That I am trying to let out
Be released from all self-pity
Inner pain and all self-doubt

May every tear my eyes shed
Turn into diamonds for my crown
May the frown that I now wear
Permanently turn back upside down

Elevation

So alone all these days,
in complete isolation.
But soon I will be seen,
this is God's preparation.

So lonely and alone,
I'm completely separated.
But this is all a must,
I am being elevated.

I am a lightworker,
A bright being of light.
So misunderstood,
but I gave up the fight.

My energy is precious,
it's far too valuable.
I must protect myself,
from those so flammable.

Like a fire extinguisher,
I put out the fire.
I replace it with love,
then lift people higher!

That is my purpose,
the reason I'm alive.
Each day of my life,
I will continue to strive!

Potential

I'm over how the darkness
Likes to poke me and prod
I want a real good man
The one for me made by God

I'm tired of the way
Men always fill me with lies
Acting like they're kings
But they're bad boys in disguise

Promising me the world
Plus the moon and all the stars
Painting pretty pictures
Of all my dreams and fancy cars

Saying that I'm the one
But then they go out and they play
Knowing that I'm a good girl
Who will wait, not go astray

I'm so sick of empty words
That they use to make me fall
From now on you best believe
That I will never give my all

To be loved with true respect
By anyone is now essential
I finally learned my lesson
Don't be blinded by potential

Just by saying that last line
I heard a voice inside me say
Use the pain that you're experiencing
Again, right now, today

Transform it into power
And then go and help another
Rise above it and be strong
You're as amazing as your mother

Remember that men's potential
Doesn't mean he's everything
Love is found in how you feel
Not just in words or in a ring

Wait until you find the one
That makes your inner light shine brighter
Allow the pain you feel in life
Turn into wisdom and become a writer

So here I am, known as Amor
I'm Elizabeth Diana Vincenty
I don't know what I'm doing here
But I know that God sent me

So, thank you for your attention
And the support that I now feel
I'm so excited to follow my dreams
And make them all, finally, real!

Fire Always Burns

You cannot play with fire
Expecting not to burn
One day you'll understand
Cause one day you'll get your turn

I leave all of my battles
In the middle of God's hands
I do not want control
Over ANY of His plans

My love for you was true
But now I don't know how to feel
I thought I had a clue
But now I don't know what is real

Don't know if I am dreaming
Or if this really all went down
I used to feel so happy
Now I'm lost in this new frown

My time and all my thoughts
Are trapped in one direction
Got me stuck inside my head
Seeking truth in deep reflection

So for that I give you thanks
What doesn't kill me makes me stronger
All this pain you're causing me
Will make my light shine brighter, longer!

Prize

Maybe it is time
For a doctor with advice
But right now I feel safe
Writing on this small device

My little iPhone
With a program called Notes
Holding all my tears
That in fact, I bet it floats

It never does break down
It never does get flooded out
If you read through all my notes
You'll know what I am all about

I'm all about true love
About God and all good things
About shining my bright light
Through the trials that life brings

I hide away to suffer
So that others do not feel
All the pain I have inside
Because I am here to heal

I'm not here to spread fear
I am here to conquer pain
I am here to show others
How to dance under the rain

So as it rains down on me
I lick my own wounds as I rise
I'm a Leo, an Earth Angel
My inner light is just the prize

Calling on My Angels

I don't know who else,
that I need to call
My Lord, all my angels,
I call on you all

I need more help,
from you to stand tall
The weight on my back,
is making me fall

I want to survive,
and I want to succeed
I only seek to have,
the things that I need

I have grown so much,
from just a small seed
And now I'm a mom,
with two kids to feed

No job in the works,
all my faith is in God
I mean what I say,
it is not a facade

Some may understand
or think I am odd
But I am who I am,
I don't seek an applaud

My life has been tough,
with great ups and downs
More times than not,
I've masked my own frowns

I'm a lover of love,
to me true love abounds
I see God in all things,
from the heavens to these grounds

Sometimes this walk,
on this planet is tough
Please Lord God hear me,
my life has been rough

I have been uplifting,
and shining through stuff
Please help me remember,
that I am enough

Through all of life's trials,
I want to be strong
These days feel so short
and the nights feel so long

So I call for my angels
with tears through a song
As I lift up my hands,
praising Whom I belong

Forever in My Prayers

Forever you'll be missed
Forever you'll be loved
Every time I hear our song
I'll remember my beloved

The good times that we had
The stressful moments too
For the type of love we shared
I have only had with you

It doesn't matter that it's over
Or that the fun came to an end
Forever I will love you
And my light to you I send

Forever in my heart
And in my prayers too
I pray that God will always
Protect you and bless you

Slow Down

You know you are the bomb
When you have haters out there
They keep trying to be like you
But they just cannot compare

They ask you for advice
Like what you use to curl your hair
And when you say, "what is on sale"
They complain, that it's not fair

But what's not fair, is how they act
Cause what they feel, is all on them
It has nothing to do with me
It's just a personal reflection

If they would stop and take a look
Into a mirror they might see
The same thing I see in them
Cause all I see, is their beauty

I see the light in everyone
We're all made in God's image
So just relax, enjoy your life
It is not a football scrimmage

Love your life, cause life loves you
But most of all please keep in mind
It's important to love yourself
And what you seek, is what you'll find

The Light Within You
Is Powerful

Butterfly

I'm stuck in a loop
One of life and death
But through each cycle
I conquer the test

With every transformation
I'm bigger and brighter
Stronger every lifetime
One heck of a fighter

The cycle is endless
Each time a clean slate
Through every transformation
Death feels like my fate

Then suddenly like magic
I burst into a light
Spreading out my wings
Ready to take flight

A butterfly emerges
So full of life and roar
Emerged from the darkness
I suffer now, no more!

My Savior

Even when my heart
Is broken and I feel
Like I am slowly dying
And this cannot be real

I lean not on my own
Understanding but on His
I trust in God my Savior
I embrace my curls and frizz

I know my God is with me
He never leaves my side
He's my king, my Holy Father
From Him I cannot hide

Nor do I ever want to
It is Him that I seek first
Each day when I arise
I can feel my inside burst

My heart fills with love
With a gratitude so true
First thought inside my mind
Is Jesus, I love You!

Thank you for my life
For blessing me today
For loving me in such
A perfect tender way

For trusting me with love
This light I love to shine
For blessing me with two
Sweet babies I call mine!

I thank Him every day
For all He has in store
Making dreams come true
Providing all plus more

I give God all the glory
I thank Him for everything
Especially for His love
All the joy that He may bring

So put your trust in Him
His plan for you is good
He loves you and loves me
More than anyone ever could

He gave us all our strengths
To use them for His glory
So I trade my pain for power
As I share my true life story

So when others see my light
After all I have gone through
They'll know that God is real
And I hope they'll seek Him too

He is Enough

You have seen it all before
You have heard it all before
But now you'll understand
Like you never did before

For when the student's ready
The teacher will appear
Before we all wake up
We live life in false fear

We think that we know all
But what we know is not true
We must live and try to learn
Grow through what we go through

Learn the learning lesson
If we don't, it will repeat
The cycle replays itself
Never does it miss a beat

Over time you will then learn
What you are ready to accept
It will then reveal itself
But let me now go more in depth

This life that we are living
Is so hard to understand
When others do their wrong
We are so quick to reprimand

But we must express our light
In a world lost in the dark
It's a double-edged sword
While your back displays a mark

Now many are waking up
While others enjoy closed eyes
Serving their egos and their flesh
Hiding behind a big disguise

They know not what they do
They are blinded more than most
Those of us who clearly see
Must be kind and never boast

We must try to stand up tall
Live good lives, live by example
If you think you're happy now
You just wait, this is a sample

The real joy that we seek
Is only found in one place
That's the palm of God's hand
In His mighty, loving grace

Keep God first every day
In every single thing you do
He is there, so rest assured
He hears you and loves you too

He just wants you to obey
His direction and His light
He wants you to do good
Avoid all evil, do what's right

He gives us all free will
So we can have it all our way
But His ways are always better
So please hear the words I say

God is not just a religion
He is love and He is joy
He is inside every heart
Of every girl and every boy

This world that we now live in
Can make our journey feel so tough
But keep your faith in Him
He's all you need, He is enough!

I Wish You Well

Those out there who are broken
Can now no longer break me
I'm finally at a place in my life
Where I have decided to choose me

I now know that everything
All happens to me for a reason
And everything and everyone
All around may be for a season

Not everyone or everything
Is meant to be forever
Some are just my learning lessons
That are required for my endeavor

Although it's hard to say goodbye
I must release what no longer serves
I must remain around good energy
Keep my light glowing with reserves

So to those who did once break me
I forgive you but I can't forget
And as I enjoy the rest of my life
I wish you all the love you can get

Because hurt people hurt others
And broken people cause pain
I wish you well with an abundance of love
So much you never notice the rain

Unexplainable Peace

I am not the Statue of Liberty
But I do have a torch and a crown
And just like that strong monument
I hold my head high with no frown

I may not have a smile to show
But inside my smile is gleaming
With honor I hold my torch up at night
While others stay asleep while dreaming

God filled me with a light to shine
For the whole entire world to see
The words I speak are not all my own
But those of God, who flow through me

Divinely intertwined, as one, I am
With the Holy Spirit and His love
I overcome any obstacle of life
As I praise God who reigns from above

For through my praise and all my tears
God replaces my pain with His peace
It's a peace that goes beyond understanding
It's so powerful it tames the inner beast

A Message From God

My dear precious child
I am with you every day
No matter what you feel
Or what others do or say

The journey you are on
Is a part of my big plan
I'm so sorry it's been hard
And difficult to understand

But lean on Me my child
I'll fill you with My peace
Don't get confused by death
Everything must decease

But death is not the end
It's just part of the cycle
Whenever you lack strength
Call on Archangel Michael

Surrounded by your Angels
Although, yes I am too there
The love I have for you
With nothing can it compare

All I ask of you my child
Is for your faith and your trust
Seeking Me in times of need
Is not a thought, it is a must

I will always be with you
Even when the veils are torn
I have always been right there
Since the day that you were born

Your experience on Earth
Is for a short moment of time
So live your life and shine bright
The light you have inside is mine

Show kindness and spread love
Forgive and show My grace
As you wake up every day
Always first seek My face

Dress yourself in My armor
Then let Me take the wheel
I will fight your every battle
Through whatever you may feel

I have given all free will
You can only steer yourself
Your obedience and faith
Will result in higher wealth

For there is a great abundance
Of the things that you desire
So stay focused on My love
I will sustain your inner fire

Confidant

You must be very careful
With the words that you use
Self-talk is so important
We unknowingly self-abuse

Like they say our minds
Are just one big battlefield
Self-destruction is a curse
So be sure to that you yield

Today, look in the mirror
And smile at who you see
Look deep into your eyes
Say: I love you endlessly

You are a true creator
You can have what you want
Don't tell yourself otherwise
Be your best confidant

Hate That I Cry

I often used to hate,
the fact that I cry.
Until one day I kneeled,
and asked my God, "WHY?"

"Why do I cry,
so much in this life?"
"Why do I always,
end up with some strife?"

Then suddenly I heard,
the voice of God say,
"My child, you will
understand it one day.

For now, all I can
really tell you is this,
I didn't give you life,
simply for fun and bliss.

I gave you this life,
because I can trust you;
And I know you will,
do what I ask of you!

I created that heart,
you hold in your chest,
And it's one of my favorites;
one of my best!

It's formed with the power,
I have in my hands!
The pain that you feel,
is part of my plans!

Although it may be tough,
to accept this hard fact,
You agreed to this journey,
and we made a pact!

The pain you go through,
is all part of your purpose.
Remember this my child,
whenever you feel nervous.

And always keep in mind,
that I am with you!
And yes, your mom and dad,
are still with you too!"

With tears in my eyes,
I thanked Him for His love.
And for always being with me,
even from up above!

So now, when I lose
self-control and I cry,
I don't waste my time
by asking God, Why?

I now take the stand
and make my light seen!
I hold my head high!
I have a crown, I'm a queen!

There is now no need,
to ever cry another tear.
The power I have within,
is stronger than any fear!

Born to Shine

Shine bright baby girl
You were born to shine
Be exactly who you are
Any less should be a crime

You were made fearless
To leave a mark on your land
Born a queen warrior
With a power that is grand

Be aware of the darkness
That lurks in plain sight
Don't let your crown slip
Always stay ready to fight

The forces of the darkness
Are compelled to destroy you
But the light you hold within
Has more weight, I assure you

So please remain strong
For your strength is now a must
Shine your light when it is dark
For in your light you can trust

Be Wise

Wise is the one,
who has few desires!
The light you hold,
is what God admires!

Loving you is all,
your sweet soul requires!
Enjoy this journey,
before it expires!

You see the chaos,
the evil, the fires!
The end is now near,
be mindful of liars!

Wise is the one,
who humbly acquires,
The lessons of life,
before it misfires!

Ignore the doubters,
the haters, deniers!
Stay far away,
from energy vampires!

Find your tribe,
they are the high-fliers!
They glow like you,
bright like highlighters!

Don't be discouraged,
by all the defiers!
The hardships, the trials,
or all that transpires!

God is with you!
He loves glorifiers!
As to His will,
you'll have your desires!

Healing

I've had to heal my inner child
And then heal my inner teen
Heal from all the heartaches
From the pain that goes unseen

I've had to heal from losing her
Where here "Her" is my mother
I've had to heal from losing him
With "Him" being my father

I've had to heal all the wounds
That my heart has slowly gained
In all the places I've been stabbed
Subtle scars there now remain

I have spent my whole life healing
So now I'm ready for my time
I'm now here to heal another
Through the love and light I shine

For although my heart's been broken
From all the pain that I've been through
It's because of all of those cracks
That my light can shine on through

Hard Times

When going through hard times
Do just that and go on through it
Don't stay there and just dwell
The power lies in how you view it

Search for help if you need help
Or better yet, seek God and pray
God loves you and He's with you
By your side, He is every day

If He gives you what you want
See that it is His direction
But if He keeps you asking
Understand it's His protection

When life feels hard to handle
Find your center in God's word
There is power and life in it
To help you soar just like a bird

You were made to shine
To maintain a high vibration
So grow through what you go through
Enjoy life like a vacation

Infinite Possibilities

Your life has eternal
Infinite possibilities
Follow your heart
Your talent and abilities

Reach for the moon
And shine with other stars
Your heart is now healed
All you have now are scars

All that you went through
Was to help you prepare
For the life soon to be
For all things will be fair

Use your discernment
Stay open and diverse
Trust God is in control
Of the whole universe

God's Plan

I know that no one's perfect
But you're perfect just for me
I know that life can be real hard
But in time, I know you'll see

That everything that happens
Is not just happening to you
In fact, it's all in perfect order
The way God intended to do

Just trust in Him and His plan
Because He knows what He's doing
He's lining up the pieces of life
To make it worth pursuing

So keep your eyes on Him
Don't let love make you blind
God wants you to have abundance
With a beautiful and sound mind

Pruned

I asked The Lord to help me
Now He's pruning my life
He's filling me with joy
And removing the strife

His love is like a quilt
A cover of good grace
I love the way He cares
Wiping tears off my face

He keeps my heart safe
With the Armor of God
He keeps me well protected
With His staff and His rod

He leads me on my path
While I walk on this earth
He watches from above
Every day since my birth

He fills me with His love
Which then turns into light
He made me who I am
A glowing star to shine bright

Sitting in Reflection

God made me with pure intention
I'm not the sum of outside rejection
All that is, is God's protection
I finally made the Divine connection

The Holy Spirt gave me the correction
After so much inner introspection
I have learned about self-affection
Low self-esteem, is like a bad infection

It quickly steers you in the wrong direction
Fears and tears become a collection
Your own home turns into a detention
Until you surrender to God in confession

His love is pure and His plans are perfection
Enjoy the dance of His interconnection
There's nothing like it, it heals all depression
And every ailment in this dimension

So remember, He made you with pure intention
You're not the sum of outside rejection
Remember it's God's way of giving protection
Be still and allow the Divine intervention

Made in His image, we are an extension
He gave us all talent as ways of expression
So follow your heart and accept imperfection
You are worth it, there is no exception

I write to self heal not for some attention
Poetry and rhythms are my way of expression
The emotions I have stuck in my possession
All turn into art as I exude in reflection

Love Me Right

Love is my answer.
Love for me is the only way.
Soft tender love.
The kind that always knows what to say.

The kind that makes you feel seen,
when you feel misunderstood.
The kind that goes out of their way,
to do whatever they possibly could.

The kind that soothes your fire,
like a breeze on a hot summer day.
The kind that makes you forget about
your troubles in every way.

The kind that never does anything,
to ever make you cry.
The kind that's always honest and,
who dares to never lie.

The kind that brings home flowers,
on a random average day.
Just because he loves how you,
light up in every way.

So, please, just love me softly,
I don't like that "tough love" thing.
A broken heart and more sad tears,
for me, is what it'll bring.

And I can't let that happen,
I can't let you dim my light.
So, if you're going to love me, then…
Please! Just, love me right.

Relax

Take a deep breath
Relax and let go
Let my love consume you
And go with the flow

The essence of my love
Is one you've never known
Just one taste of it
And you'll be mind blown

With my words I make love
Through my intellectual mind
The healing touch in my hands
Will help you relax and unwind

With me you will soon notice
The best moments that we share
Will be the ones with no words
Just God's essence in the air

Valedictorian

The mind is not to be filled
This is something I have learned
It is meant to be kindled
Like a fire to be burned

So let that fire burn
Allow the charcoals to glow bright
You are meant to shine
That is why you hold the light

Don't let others convince you
That it's okay to let it dim
Because that's a straight up lie
Just to benefit her or him

But I know you're much smarter
At the top of the whole class
Just like a valedictorian
A heart of gold, though they see brass

Just stay above the chaos
The noisy world is so distracting
Remember all you have learned
And avoid overreacting

Time

Time is ticking quickly
You must live with no regret
Be true to yourself
Remember, don't forget

You are a child of God
All things come with a reason
People come and go
Some are only for a season

You must follow your heart
Be brave enough to fail
Do the things you love to do
Enjoy the journey, every trail

Chase the dreams you have
Use your imagination
Trust God is always good
He's the author of creation

Fly

I have wings to spread
I was born to fly
Not to crawl or slither
Not to ball up and cry

I am the whole universe
Experiencing itself
But no one understands
So I just stay to myself

I am always evolving
Growing every day
God gave me this life
To be happy in every way

So from this day forward
I will be much stronger
It's time to dry my eyes
Allow tears to fall no longer

For I am now awake
My time in slumber, is now done
For my name has been called
I am Amor, the chosen one

Fine Line

It's a real fine line
Between loving and hate
I want what I want
But only if it's my fate

I want to constantly
Hold a positive state
Be filled with so much joy
I just want to feel great

I've wasted so much time
Looking for the right mate
With my hopes up too high
Even on the first date

But now I understand
It is never too late
But first of all I must
Make some room on my plate

I must keep all I can
Release all that I hate
I'm on my way to greatness
If I stay at this rate

Triggered Again

When you are triggered
Allow yourself to feel
Going through a purge
Allows yourself to heal

It's not a sentence
To suffer from the past
It's just a slow process
Don't take it too fast

Do the work that's needed
To heal your inner child
Allow yourself to cry
So emotions don't run wild

The past is not your fault
So do not stay right there
The grip it has on you
Is so strong and it's not fair

You have to take a stand
To break away from it
And believe in yourself
So you do not plummet

New Ways

I used to just assume
Brace myself for the worst
Like if life was a dream
A bubble ready to burst

I became insecure
Always doubtful, on edge
But I'm done with all that
I have new ways, I pledge

My sole focus right now
Is my emotion and mood
All things that steal my joy
Will be discarded and booed

This shadow work is hard
It's profound and just wild
All alone in solitude
With my hurt inner child

But enough is enough
It is time that I heal
Time to love who I am
Through whatever I feel

My Birthday

The evil forces of this world
Tried to stop me at my birth
They tried to cut off all my air
As they knew of my great worth

They knew that I was special
So they tried to take me out
But I was saved by my Angels
They were there with me, no doubt

But how could they do that?
My little face swollen and blue
My body was so limp
But I was stronger than they knew

The doctors quickly revived me
Then I took a few deep breaths
God then gave me power to heal
And save others from the darkness

Torch

I hold a torch of flame
It's been passed down to me
For many generations
It's been burning endlessly

One day a curse was placed
It was put upon the handle
So whoever holds the torch
Will slowly melt just like a candle

But not me, I will not melt
I've been sent by Jesus Christ
He crowned me as a queen
With a crown that's gold and iced

He built me with His armor
With a heart that holds His light
No matter what the issue is
I am here to win the fight

To reclaim the family throne
Our blood is grand and royal
God trusts me with this task
So to Him I'll remain loyal

Snakes

Be careful of the snakes
Who slither in disguise
Like the serpent in the garden
A snake is full of lies

Speaking of the serpent
Let's switch our gears a bit
Let's talk about the Bible
And the benefits of it

The stories in the Bible
Make lots of sense today
Read and pay attention
It's a book that shows the way

It's full of tiny clues
That will help you through your life
The tricks of the trade
To live life without strife

It's full of so much wisdom
Its words have strength to heal
Advice and inspiration
For every way that you may feel

Don't Disobey

It's not okay
To disobey
God wants you
To live in a way

That pleases Him
In every way
With grace for all
Good things to say

God is the light
The truth, the way
Be more like Him
And just obey

It's not okay
To disobey
The Lord our God
In any way

Follow Your Heart

When you were young
You had big dreams
You had ideas
That flowed like streams

Those dreams and thoughts
Were not from you
They were from God
Believe! It's true!

God breathed His life
Right into you
He gave you life
With desires too

Visions and dreams
All to manifest
Not to void with doubt
But to give us the best

So follow your heart
It knows what to do
Dream big! Unashamed!
Then make them come true!

The Three C's

I maintain the three C's
That's: Cool, calm and collected
I don't ask others for much
But I demand to be respected

I am not like most others
Who are always in a rush
I take the time to listen
And your feelings I'll never brush

I give others my attention
The kind that's full and undivided
I let them speak their mind to me
Even if it sounds recited

We are all facing something
Some kind of battle in the mind
So staying cool, calm and collected
Is how you always remain kind

Writers Write

I cannot dim my light
For anyone any longer
My calling from within
Is becoming much stronger

I must be obedient
I must answer the call
I must remain strong
I must stand up tall

God sent me here
With a mission on hand
Compared to other souls
My mission is grand

The light I have within
Needs to shine brighter
I was born to love all
I was born to be a writer

And writers must write
So excuse me if I do
I've been sent here with a task
A task I'm now ready to do

Birthday Wish

To you, a Happy Birthday
May all your dreams come true
Your age doesn't matter
Or whatever you've been through

You are a child of God
And you're worth your biggest dream
I know that life's been hard
But it's not all, what it may seem

Our time here on this planet
Is just a ride through endless time
Make the best of what you have
For any mountain you can climb

Every day we are brand new
As we have a brand new start
So, my birthday wish for you
Is everything inside your heart

Power of a Single Thought

Watch your thoughts,
they become words.
Once they are said,
they cannot be undone.

Watch your words,
they turn into actions.
Be mindful especially
in front of everyone.

Watch your actions,
they turn into habits
Becoming your character,
in the long run.

Watch your character
because in due time
It creates your destiny,
which you cannot outrun.

Hello

Hello, I am love;
In Spanish, it's Amor
I am full of love,
and truly so much more

I invite you all,
to now take my hands
And then go with me,
to far distant lands

You can trust me,
for I know the way
I'll light the path,
along the whole way

I know you're hurt,
And I've been hurt too
But there's a way out,
And I can lead you

So just follow me,
and do as I do
Now say as I say,
Dreams do come true!

All you must do,
is trust in your heart
Then just do it,
focus and start

The world is now yours!
What do you want?
You can have it all,
just don't go flaunt

Remain just as is,
stay who you are
Kind and humble,
a shining bright star!

I Am Love

In a constant state of change,
I forever keep growing
Been working on myself,
keeping still and just knowing

God is good, all the time;
all the time God is good
If I could make you understand,
I most certainly would

But all I can really do,
is just stay in my lane
Show others by example,
how to live and be sane

The secret to this life,
is a matter of choice
You can pick and choose your path,
just by using your voice

Speak life into existence;
Love yourself first of all
Be kind and full of grace,
and always stand tall

The light you hold within,
has the power to heal
All you need to do now,
is believe that it's real

University

At the University of struggle,
with my professor, Mr. Pain,
I have learned how to light my fire,
even under the pouring rain.

Much better than a girl scout,
with extra badges on my vest.
I am a child of thee Most High,
shining light from East to West.

Though it took a while to get here,
It took years of trial and error.
I've spent decades healing myself,
I have wounds bandaged in terror.

All the nightmares have subsided,
quite a bit, since way back then.
The one thing I learned from it all,
Is each beginning must have an end.

Be Careful

Be careful of what you think of
You have powers inside your mind
Be careful of what you search for
Be sure you're ready for what you'll find

Be careful of what you say
The words you put into existence
Be careful of what you ask for
And the illusion behind persistence

Be careful of who you trust
Not all will have your best intention
Be careful who you spend time with
The things you give all your attention

Be careful of what you wish for
You might just get it all plus more
Be careful when you fall in love
Heartbreaks hurt to the core

Just be careful and be mindful
I will not always be here
Remember all the things I've said
And live your life in love, not fear

Fear is a Liar

I have been chosen
Completely set apart
The greatest of all time
Intricate beating heart

I am an Earth Angel
Walking amongst the sheep
Lead by The Great Shepherd
Protected as I sleep

He guides my every move
Seeks me when I'm lost
The price He paid for me
Was the ultimate true cost

The love He has for me
Makes every tear have worth
I surrendered my whole life
Accepting my rebirth

I was once just a girl
But now I'm God's vessel
With the darkness of evil
I will no longer wrestle

My focus shall remain
On the light I have within
For I can do all things
And face anything with Him

While walking through the valley
Facing shadows of my death
Fear remains a liar
Until my last breath!

I Finally Found It

No longer do I feel so lost or alone.
I have finally found the treasure!
The chest is not filled with gems or stones.
It is filled with self-love and great pleasure!

The kind of love I've been searching for
is a love that is like no other.
No one can love you, like you love yourself!
Those are the words of my mother.

She told me this so very long ago,
before she got her beautiful wings.
She taught me everything she possibly could,
and she warned me of such things.

But I was just a little girl back then,
when she stopped coming back home.
At first it felt like she abandoned me,
like she just left me all alone.

But now, I'm grown and I understand,
what then really happened to her.
She got very sick and then she died,
despite what all the details were.

She was so young, such an awesome mom
and what happened to her is so crazy!
I will always keep her memory alive
and remember the love that she gave me.

And now that I am a mother myself,
I want to be a great one like her!
So now each day, I pray to God
and then listen for His whisper.

Message From My Angel

My dear precious daughter
I know you're sad I'm gone
I watch you while you sleep at night
Each day from dusk till dawn

And all throughout the days
I am right there by your side
I've been wiping all your tears
Each time that you have cried

I know you're facing a lot
It's all hard to comprehend
It's okay to show your feelings
Being strong doesn't mean pretend

When you miss me, close your eyes
Remember when I was there
Whenever you lay your head down to rest
I'll be there to caress your hair

I still hold you close and tight
Even though you do not feel me
For I will always be with you
Forever, for all eternity

Grateful Either Way

I think in a whole new different way
And now it's coming into play
I'm lost for words, nothing to say
I hate that we're stuck in this grey

So tell me some nice things today
Help me to smile in some way
Because if you ask, I will then say
That, all is well, yes I'm okay

But if you read my book one day
You then will see things in my way
You'll see how I live everyday
And why I still cry in some way

Yes I am blessed in many ways
But I still face things on most days
I'm grateful either way this plays
I thank God for life, all my days!

Glory be to God

I only want to have
What glorifies you
I only want to say
What will glorify you

I only want to be
What glorifies you
I only want to go
Where it glorifies you

Everything in my mind
May it glorify you
Everything that I do
May it glorify you

Every turn that I take
May it glorify you
May my life itself be
One that glorifies you

God's Armor

Be careful what you think of
You have powers in your mind
Relax and just be still
The Lord is good all of the time

Just keep your faith in Him
It's not in your time nor mine
Leave it all in God's hands
In His Divinely perfect time

Don't let the devil fool you
He loves to steal your shine
He slowly lurks and hides from us
Standing off on the sideline

Waiting for the right moment
When our guards start to decline
So be sure to put on God's whole armor
Because you were born to shine

Dear Angels

Dear angels of mine,
please help me to see.
Those who are out there,
who are against me.

Please protect me,
more than ever before.
I'm starting to understand,
that I am so much more.

I'm more than this body,
I'm more than my name.
I was born for greatness,
for stardom and fame.

But evil dark forces,
keep trying hard to win.
I can feel the cold pull,
with temptation of sin.

Please guide me through,
all the valleys of hell.
Lead me to triumph,
to rest and to dwell.

Right at the feet,
of my Heavenly Father.
I promise to be good,
and never a bother.

I know I still have,
a very long way to go.
But I'm doing so well,
and I'm on a good flow!

So please help me Angels,
I need your protection.
Help me to remain,
within God's true perfection!

Golden Hour

Cotton candy clouds
Sun-kissed warm sky
Gazing upon the heavens
With a twinkle in my eye

This very time of the day
Is my favorite and by far
I love how it all looks
Before the sky is full of stars

I love the different colors
That spread across the sky
And how the voice of God
Seems to slowly amplify

A pretty blue to my left
That softly fades to white
Then into the prettiest of pinks
When you look out to the right

It never does get old
I love watching the sunset
When the air begins to crisp
That's the best feeling yet

Ask-firmations

I found the true secret,
behind an affirmation
If you're looking for a sign,
this is your confirmation

Instead of just affirming,
change it to a question
This is a new command,
it isn't a suggestion

When you just affirm,
there is still some resistance
Be patient with yourself,
it takes time and persistence

Rest assured it is working,
It is not a competition
No need for a reward,
accolades or recognition

All you need is to relax,
and believe in who you are
Ask yourself a simple question,
like "Am I a shining star?"

The brain is like a friend,
who wants to seek for a solution
Once you ask it a question,
soon you'll have a resolution

Bridge

I can heal your pain,
but I need your sole belief
God made me the bridge,
from suffering to relief

Allow me to lead you,
away from all the pain
I have a gold umbrella,
I'll keep you from the rain

I hold a torch of fire,
that illuminates the path
I'm like a liaison,
between you and God's wrath

The chambers of my heart,
All illuminate with light
The power I have within,
Is enough to win the fight

The light inside my heart,
Fiercely bursts through all the cracks
My pain is now my power,
I'm just giving you the facts

I agreed to choose this path,
And all the pain this time around
The heartaches that I've had,
All drove my face into the ground

The tears that I have wept,
Were collected in God's hands
He turned them into diamonds,
as I obeyed all his commands

So now when I go home,
and I then join the Angel army
I will have my beautiful wings
and my crown will be placed on me

An Angel with Wings

I'm an angel on earth
An earth angel with wings
About to spread them wide
Blessed by the King of all Kings

My mission on this earth
Is to shine and to heal
To help uplift humans
Through the things that they feel

Some will understand me
But most others will not
Some days I feel so strong
While other days, I feel shot

But no matter how I feel
I get up and I keep trying
If I told you it was easy
To you I'd secretly be lying

New Day

It's a brand-new day, the sun has come up
So it's time to take a moment and to pray
I say, "Good morning God, thank You for life
And for the blessing of this brand-new day"

"God, please go before me in every way,
Please guide all my words and actions.
May the Holy Spirit fill me in a way,
That allows me to control my reactions"

For the way I react is misunderstood
I'm judged and right away, I am wrong
It's amazing how it's so quickly forgotten
Who I am; where I been, and how I'm strong

But it's all good, the opinions of others
Don't affect me like they once did before
I'm stronger than ever with the Armor of God
I feel safe and I fear now no more

So when life feels heavy or overwhelming
Give all of your worries to The Lord
He will fill you with everlasting strength
And inner peace as the ultimate reward

Inner Beast

I can feel my inner beast
Slowly rising to the surface
Both eyelids squinted low
With my mindset on my purpose

All the pieces of my heart
Are now gathered in my hand
The fragments are so small
Like the size of beach sand

When a glass simply breaks
You can glue it back together
But with pieces as small as sand
Restoration will be never

All that's left now to be done
Is for the Potter to recreate
Let Him mold you into new
Although a lion is your fate

So let your inner beast now roar
Let out your hurt and all your pain
Then go rest for what's to come
For sunshine comes after the rain

In God's Hands

I leave all of my battles
In the palm of God's hands
I do not want control
Over any of His plans

His plans for me are greater
Than all that I can see
Even when I feel alone
I know that He is there with me

My thoughts and all my dreams
Are just a taste of what's in store
The purpose of my life
Is rooting up and out my core

The day that I arrived
Was the day a star was born
With a mission set in stone
For the day the veil is torn

I Pray to You

Lord I love You, it's You who's in me
So I shine my light as bright as can be
It's You who I honor and give the glory
You are my whole world, the one who made me

I give you my heart and all of my soul
I pray that you heal me and make me whole
Surrendered to You, I want You in control
The ways I once was has taken its toll

No longer do I want to cry all these tears
Life is too short to waste any more years
I'm ready to fly and then see what appears
Before time is up and my chance disappears

So I bow my head and I pray now to you
I ask that you hear me and do what you do
I know that you love me and I love you too
My heart may be broken but You are my glue

Put me together in Your perfect new way
So You get the glory for what I may say
I praise You and thank You for life every day
It's in the name of Jesus mighty name that I pray

Thank You

I truly want to thank you,
And you know just who you are
The distance doesn't matter
Whether if we're near or far

We pick up where we finished
From the last time that we met
Every time we share a visit
It's so good we can't forget

How long it ever goes
The transition is so smooth
Never any awkwardness
With the time our hearts soothe

We're all about the quality
Quantity is overrated
The friendship that we have
Is one Divinely orchestrated

So I thank you for your love
I thank God for you each day
The kind of love you've shown to me
Makes me love you in every way!

Milton Keynes UK
Ingram Content Group UK Ltd.
UKHW020753051024
449151UK00012B/563